If We Were Birds

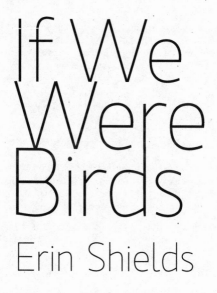

If We Were Birds

Erin Shields

Playwrights Canada Press
Toronto

PLAYWRIGHTS CANADA PRESS
The Canadian Drama Publisher
215 Spadina Ave., Suite 230, Toronto, ON Canada M5T 2C7
phone 416.703.0013 fax 416.408.3402
info@playwrightscanada.com • www.playwrightscanada.com

For professional or amateur production rights, please contact:
Charles Northcote, Core Literary Inc.
140 Wolfrey Ave., Toronto, ON M4K 1L3
phone 416.466.4929, email charlesnorthcote@rogers.com

Playwrights Canada Press acknowledges the financial support of the Government of Canada through the Canada Book Fund and the Canada Council for the Arts and of the Province of Ontario through the Ontario Arts Council and the Ontario Media Development Corporation, for our publishing activities.

Canada Council   Conseil des Arts   ONTARIO ARTS COUNCIL
for the Arts   du Canada   CONSEIL DES ARTS DE L'ONTARIO

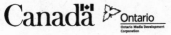

Cover by sandwich creative

LIBRARY AND ARCHIVES CANADA CATALOGUING IN PUBLICATION
Shields, Erin
If we were birds / Erin Shields.

Play.
Based on one of Ovid's Metamorphoses, "Tereus, Procne and Philomela".
Also issued in electronic formats.
ISBN 978-1-77091-012-6

I. Title.

PS8637.H497I3 2011   C812'.6   ·   C2011-904313-0

First edition: August 2011
Second printing: December 2011
Printed and bound in Canada by Gauvin Press, Gatineau

For Gideon Arthurs.

And for all those women who survived the unspeakable
and still continue to fly.

A Note on the Chorus

These characters are inspired by testimonials of women survivors from the following conflicts: Nanking (1937), Berlin (1945), Bangladesh (1971), Bosnia-Herzegovina (1992–1995) and Rwanda (1994). Each character relates to a particular conflict and incorporates details from many stories. It is not my intention for an audience to match the conflict to the character, but rather to experience a diverse chorus of contemporary women who have suffered sexual violence enacted as a weapon of war. Casting should be as diverse as possible in terms of race, age, body type and voice. Their physicality should be bird-like as the Chorus and human as the Slave Women and Servants.

If We Were Birds was first produced at the Tarragon Theatre in association with Groundwater Productions from April 14–May 23, 2010 with the following cast and crew:

Philomela: Tara Rosling
Procne: Philippa Domville
Pandion: David Fox
Tereus: Geoffrey Pounsett
The Young One: Stephanie Jung
The Pregnant One: Daniela Lama
The Bleeding One: Shannon Perreault
The Pious One: Karen Robinson
The One with Dwindling Dignity: Barbara Gordon

Directed by Alan Dilworth
Assistant direction by Kristina Nicoll
Set and costume design by Jung-Hye Kim
Lighting design by Kimberly Purtell
Sound and composition by Thomas Ryder Payne
Movement coaching by Allyson McMackon
Fight direction by Simon Fon
Stage managed by Kristen Kitcher
Apprentice stage management by Shelby-Jai Donkers
Script coordinated by Julia Pileggi

A workshop production of *If We Were Birds* was staged at the SummerWorks Theatre Festival in 2008, produced by Groundwater Productions.

Punctuation Note

A slash (/) indicates a point at which the following line cuts in early, creating overlap.

Characters

Philomela—Younger daughter of King Pandion
Procne—Older daughter of King Pandion
King Pandion—King of Athens
King Tereus—King of Thrace

Slave Women—A group of women captured in battle by Tereus, given as a gift to King Pandion, played by the Chorus (shorthand—Bleeding SW, etc.)
Itys—Son of Procne and Tereus played by the Bleeding One and a piece of white cloth
Servant—Servant to Procne played by the Bleeding One

The Chorus—A chorus of ravaged women who have been transformed into birds by the gods

The Young One
The Pregnant One
The Bleeding One
The Pious One
The One with Dwindling Dignity

Prologue — Nature

PHILOMELA and the CHORUS dwell in a timeless purgatory of nature. They scavenge and are hunted. In darkness:

CHORUS   *(whispered)* Speak it, speak it, speak it, speak.

Lights up on PHILOMELA wrapped in a blanket of feathers. Seeing the audience, she opens her mouth and blood spills down her chin.

PHILOMELA   The gods have sewn my tongue back in.
Some sort of mercy for some sort of guilt,
and they'll be wanting some sort of praise.
Thanks.
Now that it's back, it cowers in the depths of my throat,
curled and trembling,
remembering the squeeze of pincers
so I need to coax it forward to speak.
Like this:

She sticks out her tongue. The CHORUS makes sounds of approval. Lights slowly up on the CHORUS wrapped in blankets of feathers.

I think they've sewn it back so I can sing through the night;
so I can mourn my fate with a sweet sweet song.
No more silence, thanks to Aphrodite.
Was it her guilt that brought me back
to the world of the more-than-screaming?

CHORUS   *(whispered)* Speak it, speak it, / speak it, speak it, speak it, speak it—

PHILOMELA   Not much has changed, now that I'm a bird.
                Especially the size of my fear:
                large enough to get caught in the throat but not enough to die.

CHORUS   Speak it, speak it, / speak it, speak it—

PHILOMELA   We were born for fear because the gods made us weak,
                but when we were girls we could run as fast,
                jump as high, yell as loud as the boys,
                so you can see why we forgot to shake.

                The CHORUS shutters, shivers and cowers.

CHORUS   Speak it, speak it, speak it / speak it—

PHILOMELA   Before the fear.

CHORUS   Yes?

PHILOMELA   Oh, before the fear we...

CHORUS   Yes?

PHILOMELA   We moved in such different ways.
                When we were children, Procne and I,
                we would disappear for hours
                through a maze of closets and tunnels calling:
                "Marco!"

                PROCNE enters.

PROCNE   "Polo!"

PHILOMELA   "Marco!"

PROCNE   "Polo!"

BOTH	We were not frightened of darkness then.
PROCNE	We were not nervous with lightning bugs or spiders.
PHILOMELA	We could pick up critters —
PROCNE	In the palms of our hands; construct intricate homes for them in jars —
PHILOMELA	Or cardboard boxes.
CHORUS, PHILOMELA, PROCNE	We were not frightened of darkness then.
PHILOMELA	And I could hold my breath for longer than you in the bath.

Scene 1 — Bathtub Talk

The CHORUS forms the bathtub in which PHILOMELA and PROCNE bathe. PHILOMELA is underwater.

PROCNE	Eighty-one, eighty-two, eighty-three, eighty-four, eighty-five —

PHILOMELA gasps for air.

PHILOMELA	How long?
PROCNE	Seventy-two seconds.
PHILOMELA	One shy of your record.
PROCNE	You'll never beat me.
PHILOMELA	Again.
PROCNE	I'm bored.

PHILOMELA   What now?

PROCNE   Three questions you'd only ask in the bath.

PHILOMELA   What's your favourite birdsong?

PROCNE   You'd only ask about birdsong in the bath?

PHILOMELA   Father isn't fond of birds.

PROCNE   Come on.

PHILOMELA   He shoots them through the window.

PROCNE   Boring.

PHILOMELA   All right.

PROCNE   All right.

PHILOMELA   Anything?

PROCNE   As long as it's good.

PHILOMELA   What is it that bulges out from under a soldier's tunic?

PROCNE   Philomela!

PHILOMELA   You said anything.

PROCNE   I'm glad you asked.

PHILOMELA   All right.

PROCNE   All right.

PHILOMELA   Go on.

PROCNE   It is a fleshy utensil.

PHILOMELA   A fleshy utensil?

PROCNE   Yes.

PHILOMELA   Oh.

PROCNE   Next question.

PHILOMELA   What's it for?

PROCNE   Dirty mind!

PHILOMELA   You told me to ask.

PROCNE   It is the fleshy utensil that contains a man's ambition in love.

PHILOMELA   Well that's disappointing.

PROCNE   Why?

PHILOMELA   I thought Aphrodite shot men in the heart.

PROCNE   She does.

PHILOMELA   Then how can the fleshy utensil be ambition in love?

PROCNE   It's all connected.

PHILOMELA   What?

PROCNE   Just listen.

PHILOMELA   I am.

PROCNE   Men are shot through the heart, then their ambition grows.

PHILOMELA   It grows?

PROCNE   And gets firm.

PHILOMELA   Firm?

PROCNE   Like a sac filled with wine.

PHILOMELA   Really?

PROCNE   Of course.

PHILOMELA   And then girls get to drink from the sac filled with wine?

PROCNE   Philomela!

PHILOMELA   I'll burst one open, kneel underneath and drink until it runs down my face.

PROCNE   That's disgusting.

PHILOMELA   You're disgusting.

PROCNE   Next question.

PHILOMELA   So what contains my ambition in love?

PROCNE   It's not the same for girls.

PHILOMELA   But I must have a—

PROCNE   Do you see a fleshy utensil flopping between your thighs!

PHILOMELA   Right here.

PROCNE   Don't touch that.

PHILOMELA   Why?

PROCNE   Just leave it alone.

PHILOMELA   Why?

PROCNE   Next / question.

PHILOMELA   Do you touch it?

PROCNE   What?

PHILOMELA   That little bit. Do you touch it?

PROCNE   Of course not.

PHILOMELA   I'll bet you do.

PROCNE   Stop it.

PHILOMELA   This is bathtub talk.

PROCNE   Yes.

PHILOMELA   My question is good. Do you touch it?

PROCNE   This isn't the / type of question—

PHILOMELA   Open your legs and wiggle it back and forth, back and forth, back and forth—

PROCNE   I...

PHILOMELA   You have to be honest.

PROCNE   I know.

PHILOMELA   Do you do it?

PROCNE   Now and again. All right? I do it too.

                Beat.

PHILOMELA   You do?

PROCNE   Well, yes.

                Beat.

PHILOMELA   I never said I did it.

PROCNE   What?

PHILOMELA   You said, "I do it too." Well I never said I did it. I can't
                wait to tell father.

PROCNE   You little shit!

                *PROCNE dunks PHILOMELA's head underwater and holds her
                down. PHILOMELA squirms free. The bathtub opens up into
                their room as they dry off.*

PHILOMELA   I wouldn't tell.

PROCNE   If you did, I'd hold you down longer than eighty-five
                seconds.

PHILOMELA   You counted seventy-two.

PROCNE   I counted eighty-five.

PHILOMELA   I did win. Eighty-five. Now I get a promise.

PROCNE   One promise.

PHILOMELA   You must swear to tell everything about fleshy utensils
                and their uses after you marry.

PROCNE   I will.

PHILOMELA   Swear it.

PROCNE   On our mother below.

Beat.

PHILOMELA   I don't want you to leave.

PROCNE   I won't leave.

PHILOMELA   But when you marry.

PROCNE   He'll live here.

PHILOMELA   Maybe not.

PROCNE   Maybe not.

PHILOMELA   Then I will follow you.
Wherever you go.
I'll sneak out of the palace dressed as a boy,
steal a ship and brave the horrid torrents of the sea,
and even if my sails rip and I'm tossed adrift,
I'll be a daughter of Triton.
I can hold my breath for eighty-five seconds
and that's how long it will take for me
to reach your shore.
I tell you, I'll reach your shore.

PHILOMELA and PROCNE exit.

Scene 2 — An Ode to Virginity

The CHORUS cleans up the mess from the bathtub.

CHORUS   We give praise to Hymen,

PREGNANT   great god of marriage;

YOUNG   the maker and preserver of virginity fair.

BLEEDING   Thank you, dear Hymen,
              for placing my hymen in a place to be ripped
              by the first man to enter me fully.

PIOUS   My blood is a gift I can give to my husband
              on our first night alone:
              evidence of my purity, my innocence, my love.

YOUNG   Thank you oh Hymen for bestowing upon me this valued charm
              so when it's stolen from me everyone will know.

DWINDLING   Thank you Hymen for making me the protector
              of my delicate virginity.
              I guard it like a lion, like a wolf, like a lamb.

YOUNG   Because my hymen is the worst thing I could lose.

DWINDLING   It isn't like a foot,

PIOUS   if lost I cannot walk.

DWINDLING   It isn't like a hand,

YOUNG   if lost I cannot work.

DWINDLING   It isn't like my eyes,

BLEEDING   if lost I cannot find my way.

DWINDLING   If I lose my virginity I cannot...

CHORUS   Yes?

DWINDLING   I cannot be...

CHORUS   Yes?

DWINDLING   I cannot use...

CHORUS   Well?

PREGNANT   Oh thank you Hymen for making me accountable
for a thin layer of skin.
I promise I have the strength not to let anyone
but my husband in.

The CHORUS sets the next scene then steps into the shadows to watch.

Scene 3 — A Celebrated Battle

King PANDION sits in his throne room in Athens. TEREUS enters.

PANDION   Come in come in come in come in.

TEREUS   Sir.

PANDION   Welcome back, King Tereus, welcome back to Athens.

TEREUS   Thank you.

PANDION   And how did you fare with that skirmish in Thebes?

TEREUS   She is once again free of rebel invaders.

PANDION   Good job, man!
The Thebans are our most valued trading partners
so it was wise of me to ask you to come to their defence.
Aren't I wise! Ha ha!

TEREUS   Ha ha! Sir.

PANDION   All right. Give us a story then.

TEREUS   A story?

PANDION   Of the battle, man. The battle!

TEREUS   Of course.

>   *TEREUS opens a game board and places tiny soldiers in position.*

PANDION   What is this marvellous thing?

TEREUS   My tactical war map.

PANDION   Splendid!

>   *TEREUS moves his men around the board as he speaks.*

TEREUS   When I arrived with my troops,
               the walls of Thebes were beginning to crumble.
               The surrounding towns were flattened and
               rebels were clawing / at the gates —

PANDION   Only the best bits then.

TEREUS   What's that?

PANDION   Of the battle. The juicy bits, you know. My dinner's on
               the way.

TEREUS   Of course.
               The rebels had increased themselves
               in number, having recruited homeless buggers from sur-
               rounding villages found blubbering over a lost stew pan
               or a stolen goat.

PANDION   But those villagers were loyal to Thebes.

TEREUS   When the battle began they screamed at the walls
               but Thebes would not open her gates to save them.

PANDION   Foolish Thebans!

TEREUS   So the rebels forced the villagers to join them
                and we had to fight them both.

PANDION   Don't spare any detail.

TEREUS   Very well.

PANDION   But be mindful of my dinner.

TEREUS   I mobilized my men here, at the southern gates,
                then with Ares pulsing through our blood
                we bashed ribs and skulls and hips and faces,
                spraying the walls of Thebes with rebel innards.

PANDION   Tell me, did you sever any heads?

TEREUS   Too many to count.

PANDION   Using one swoop? Or does it generally take two or three?

TEREUS   Depends on the man.

PANDION   Thickness of his neck and all that.

TEREUS   Of course.

PANDION   What about my neck, then.

TEREUS   What about it?

PANDION   How many blows do you think?

TEREUS   Sir?

PANDION   To chop off my head?

                PANDION bares his neck. TEREUS examines it.

TEREUS   I'd say at least five or six.

PANDION   Now here's a warrior's neck, eh.
             Too bad Athens is so large.
             I tell you I'd be out on the battlefield
             if it weren't for all this paper—
             administration and all that.

TEREUS   Such a shame, sir.
             I'd love to see you out in the field.

PANDION   Yes, yes, the field.
             Out in the field, back to back, you and I,
             I can see it now, chopping one head after the next,
             swooping to one another's defence
             in the heat of the mid-afternoon.
             Then at night, with sweat and blood of the day
             on our backs and cheeks,
             stretched out under the stars, you and I,
             I can see us, smiling up at the gods.

             Would you mind if I held your soldier's bride?

TEREUS   My soldier's bride?

PANDION   You know, your blade. Your dagger, your dragonforce.

TEREUS   Sir?

PANDION   Your Peter the Great, your pork, your ninja, your purple-
             headed yogourt slinger.

TEREUS   My sword?

PANDION   Any hero would be honoured for the king of Athens to
             grip onto his legend.

TEREUS   Of course.

PANDION   If only for a moment.

TEREUS reluctantly hands over his sword. PANDION has trouble lifting it, but then starts waving it about in mock battle.

PANDION   Solid iron, this.

TEREUS   Plated with gold, forged by Hephaestus.

PANDION   My grandfather, you know.

TEREUS   Careful there, sir.

PANDION   I have five in my bedroom. All gold-plated. Ha!

PANDION lunges with the sword, TEREUS ducks out of his way.

TEREUS   Good one, sir.

PANDION continues to wave the sword about while TEREUS pretends to try to get out of his way.

PANDION   How were you greeted by the Theban king?

TEREUS   With moderate words of welcome,
begrudging sighs of thanks.

PANDION   Wasn't he grateful?

TEREUS   Yes, grateful, yes.
But angry I'd allowed my men
to indulge in the spoils of war.

PANDION   The spoils?

TEREUS   In the evenings when we flopped in the rubble
of Thebes' surrounding villages,
my men feasted on wandering goats
and satisfied themselves with displaced women.

PANDION   Well that is every soldier's right.
               In times of war, and all that.
               If we had to pay soldiers in gold,
               our coffers would be empty.

TEREUS   Yes.

PANDION   Empty! Ha!

> *PANDION brings the sword down upon the game board and
> the little soldiers spill onto the floor.*

Well then. Huh. The sound of scattering men. Ha ha.

> *PANDION returns the sword.*

Wine! Wine!

> *Wine is brought.*

To you, King Tereus, son of Ares.
May the gods always favour your sword,
and may you always favour the kingdom of Athens.

> *TEREUS gulps back his wine.*

Are you all right, man?

TEREUS   I have brought you a gift.

PANDION   A gift?

> *The CHORUS steps forward, becoming the SLAVE WOMEN.
> Many are bleeding, all are miserable.*

TEREUS   The spoils of war, good king.
               Now slaves to you and yours.

PANDION   But it is your right to take them to Thrace.

TEREUS	It is my right to give them to whomever I please.
PANDION	Well, thank you. Ah, they look a bit, well, used.
TEREUS	They have been travelling sixteen days by foot and by soldier but they will clean up well.
PANDION	You too shall not go unrewarded. Ah... let's see now. Huh.
TEREUS	No gift is required.
PANDION	Not required! Who do you think I am now? Hmm... Of course. Yes, yes. Girls. Girls!

PROCNE and PHILOMELA enter.

PROCNE & PHILOMELA	Yes, Father.
PANDION	Girls. My girls. You see, man. These are my girls. Spitting image of their mother. Both of them. My girls.

Beat.

Tereus, you will marry Procne, the elder of the two.

TEREUS	I couldn't possibly—
PANDION	I've decided, so that's it then.
TEREUS	Sir, I—

PANDION   Step forward, luv.
               Hold out your hand.
               I can think of no finer warrior to give my daughter to.

TEREUS   Gracious king.

PANDION   Noble friend. She is yours.

                    TEREUS takes PROCNE's hand.

TEREUS   And how will this suit you?

PROCNE   It makes me...
               I am...

PANDION   I'm proud to say she is properly inexperienced in matters
               of men.

TEREUS   Really?

PANDION   Completely uninformed.

PROCNE   I am happy to please my father.

TEREUS   Then you will be happy to please your husband.

PROCNE   Yes.

PANDION   Good girl.
               My good girl.
               We will have the ceremony tomorrow morning
               before Tereus sets sail for Thrace.

PROCNE & PHILOMELA
               For Thrace?

PHILOMELA   But a husband should move into his wife's home.

PROCNE   Philomela, don't.

PANDION	Oh my dove, not if he has a kingdom of his own.
PHILOMELA	Please, Father.
PANDION	Of course you are welcome to stay. We could train with our swords together every day.
TEREUS	My people await my return.
PHILOMELA	Can't you at least stay a month?
PANDION	That's enough out of you.
TEREUS	Your sister will have it all.
PHILOMELA	Except for me.
PROCNE	Look, Philomela, I'm happy.
PANDION	You can prepare the ritual for your sister. Give her a good farewell then.
PHILOMELA	Yes, Father.
PANDION	Procne, Tereus, let's make the announcement.

PANDION, TEREUS and PROCNE exit. PHILOMELA and the CHORUS remain.

Scene 4 — The Soldier's Defence

The SLAVE WOMEN look at PHILOMELA.

| PHILOMELA | And what are you looking at? |
| PIOUS SW | We look at Philomela. |

DWINDLING SW The daughter of a king.

PHILOMELA King Pandion of Athens.

BLEEDING SW Athens? Is that where we've been dragged?

PHILOMELA You're lucky. My father treats our slaves well.

PREGNANT SW Hopefully better than he treats his daughters.

PHILOMELA What's that supposed to mean?

PREGNANT SW Nothing, madam, nothing.

PIOUS SW You clearly don't agree.

PHILOMELA Agree with what?

DWINDLING SW That your sister fell prey to an overly hasty engagement.

PHILOMELA Oh.

PIOUS SW No meeting of parents,
no chaperoned dates,
no holding of hands.

PHILOMELA She's happy.

PIOUS SW Are you?

PHILOMELA Of course. It just happened so fast.

PREGNANT SW Will you try to stop it?

PHILOMELA What I do or don't do is no business of yours.

DWINDLING SW Would you look at the red in her cheek?

PIOUS SW I think she's a little bit flustered.

PHILOMELA   I'm not.

PIOUS SW   Can you blame her?
Losing her sister to a man like that.

PHILOMELA   A man like what?

DWINDLING SW   To a general.

PIOUS SW   A man who breeds war.

BLEEDING SW   A descendant of Ares, no less.

PHILOMELA   I admire Tereus.
He's a noble warrior.

BLEEDING SW   A mercenary.

PHILOMELA   A defender of justice:
one who can chop heads and hands from the enemy
without hesitation or remorse.

BLEEDING SW   That's just what I look for in a man.

PHILOMELA   Everyone he attacks deserves what he gets.

PREGNANT SW   Really? Did I deserve what I got?

PHILOMELA   If you hadn't done anything wrong, you wouldn't be here.

PREGNANT SW   Six soldiers came searching our home for pamphlets
in the middle of the night.

PHILOMELA   You were circulating propaganda.

PREGNANT SW   When they found there was nothing to find,
they threw my husband out of bed
and took turns with me
while one watched and one waited.

One by one they hammered my body into my skull.
My husband threw up, poor thing.
Somewhere around the fourth or fifth
I fell into unconsciousness.

My husband refuses to see me.
It was a lot for him, poor thing.

PHILOMELA   And why should I believe a woman like you?

PREGNANT SW   Don't you see how my belly has grown since that night?

PHILOMELA   You've made up a horrible story
              to excuse your indiscretion.

BLEEDING SW   Will you send your sister off with a soldier
              capable of acts like these?

PHILOMELA   If you were, as you say, attacked in the night,
              how is Tereus to blame?

PIOUS SW   Isn't he their general?

DWINDLING SW Doesn't he give the commands?

PHILOMELA   He's not responsible for everything his soldiers do.
              Besides, you were probably smuggling supplies.

PREGNANT SW   Should I strangle it, do you think?

PHILOMELA   Or you were hiding the enemy.

PREGNANT SW   Should I float it down a river?

PHILOMELA   I've heard about women like you.

DWINDLING SW Really? What have you heard?

PHILOMELA   You welcome soldiers into your beds
              then kill them while they sleep.

DWINDLING SW   Yes, you should see the blood on my pillow.

PHILOMELA   You hold meetings in your kitchens late at night.

DWINDLING SW   When the soldiers force themselves in.

PHILOMELA   You hide rebels under the floorboards
and feed them rationed supplies.

DWINDLING SW   They sleep where they fall and eat what they like.

PHILOMELA   Even old ladies can conceal the enemy.

DWINDLING SW   It's true, Philomela, I did conceal the enemy.

PHILOMELA   Ah ha! I was right. I should be an interrogator.

DWINDLING SW   I concealed my sons and grandsons
until soldiers dragged them into the streets.

PHILOMELA   Clearly they were traitors.

DWINDLING SW   I concealed my daughters and granddaughters
in shadows and cracks in the floor.
I whispered truths to the little ones
about the folded spaces between their legs
to prepare them for the unspeakable.

PHILOMELA   What do you mean?

DWINDLING SW   I didn't think to conceal myself.
It's the young they want so
I'll be the wall between war and my girls.
What would they want with me?

PHILOMELA   Soldiers don't just...
That doesn't sound like...
It can't be true.

        (to the YOUNG ONE) What about you?

PIOUS SW   She is looking for her sisters.

PHILOMELA   Were you lucky enough to catch a glimpse of the hero?

DWINDLING SW   Let the Young One alone.

PHILOMELA   Tell me what you saw.
Speak or I won't give you any lunch.

BLEEDING SW   Oh the power she wields.

DWINDLING SW   Go on, child.

PHILOMELA   Go on.

YOUNG SW   Me and my sisters were hiding in the woods.
But we went home 'cause we had nothing to eat.
At night we slept in the same bed
'cause we thought they'd leave us alone
if we were all together.
They came in wearing animal skins
and put a knife to each of my eyes
and said if I cried
they'd cut them out.

PIOUS SW   She is looking for her sisters.

PHILOMELA   Her sisters, yes, go on.

YOUNG SW   There were lights in our faces.
Our bodies in the dirt
opened twice, opened again,
rapidly, quickly.
They made me stand up
and it was hard to stand up
and it was hard to stay up.
Then we walked for hours into the woods.
Every night after that
they made a circle around me and held up my legs.

DWINDLING SW   My children and their children
cannot look me in the eye.

YOUNG SW   The villagers are ashamed.

PREGNANT SW   And my husband.

BLEEDING SW   And me.

YOUNG SW   Have you seen my sisters?

PREGNANT SW   Should I drown it, do you think?

YOUNG SW   I lost them in the woods.

DWINDLING SW   Is this what my family deserved?

PIOUS SW   I prayed they would leave us alone.

YOUNG SW   Have you seen my sisters?

PREGNANT SW   Do you want to take it?

CHORUS SW   Is this your glorious war?

PHILOMELA cries.

BLEEDING SW   Now she overflows.

YOUNG SW   She understands our pain.

PHILOMELA   My sister will leave tomorrow and I will be alone.

PIOUS SW   It is not our pain that grieves her,
but her own silly plight.

DWINDLING SW   Poor girl, alone;
alone in the house of a father who loves her too much.

PHILOMELA   I'll have no one to talk to but slaves.

PREGNANT SW   We were not always slaves.

PHILOMELA   Enough!

    Beat.

I need to be brave for my sister,
to help her prepare for the wedding.

    PHILOMELA goes to PROCNE. The SLAVE WOMEN morph
    back into birds to watch the girls.

Scene 5 — Bind Us Together

    PHILOMELA dresses PROCNE. PROCNE tries to remember the
    details of the wedding ceremony. PHILOMELA holds a scroll
    with instructions.

PROCNE   So first I take the basket.

PHILOMELA   The basket of the untouched virgin.

PROCNE   Right. Basket of the untouched virgin. Right. I do a prayer
for Athena at the top of the Acropolis.

PHILOMELA   Then you walk—

PROCNE   Down the secret steps.

PHILOMELA   Down to the garden of Aphrodite.

PROCNE   Goddess of everything.

PHILOMELA   Goddess of everything stroked and rubbed and wet.

PROCNE

Stroked and...
Stroked and...
Oh gods.
I can't do this.

PHILOMELA

It's easy:
stroked and rubbed and wet.

PROCNE

Not that—this.

PHILOMELA

But you've been practising for years.
You've done this ritual, this wedding, this night alone
a million times.

PROCNE

With you.

PHILOMELA

Exactly.

PROCNE

It's not the same.

PHILOMELA

Pretend it is.

PROCNE

No.

PHILOMELA

Why not? I'm just as valiant as Tereus.
"Grrrrr, here I am fresh from battle.
Grrrr, I've chopped off heads."

PROCNE

Stop it.

PHILOMELA

"See the blood dripping from my shoulders!"

PROCNE

Disgusting.

PHILOMELA

"And the hands hanging from my belt!
Who is the woman that comes to be my bride?"

PROCNE

Stop it.

PHILOMELA   I said, "Who is the woman that comes to be my bride?"

PROCNE   "Here I am, fresh from the garden."

PHILOMELA   "Put out your hand."

PROCNE   "But you might chop it off."

PHILOMELA   "Not if it pleases me."

PROCNE puts out her hand.

"Hmmmm, nice-sized wrist. Not too boney, not too fleshy."

PROCNE   "I will give you many sons."

PHILOMELA   "Then bind us, priest, bind us together."

PROCNE   "Bind us, priest, bind us together."

PHILOMELA   "Now you can look at my fleshy utensil."

They burst into laughter.

See, it's easy.

PROCNE   You make it easy because you don't know.

PHILOMELA   I know as much as you.

PROCNE   You don't know about this clenching in my stomach.

PHILOMELA   You should be excited.

PROCNE   Excitement isn't a real feeling for anyone but a child.

PHILOMELA   I'm not a child.

PROCNE   You are.

PHILOMELA   You're the one who's whining.

PROCNE   I think marriage is like death: we consume ourselves in imagining what's on the other side and then all at once we're there.

PHILOMELA   Then shouldn't you enjoy the crossing over?

PROCNE   My head is ready for it; right here floating above my body, reciting the ritual, the words, the actions like everything we've done before. But then down here...

PHILOMELA   Where?

PROCNE   There's this churning, a wave of something I've never felt and it's pushing into my mind, distracting me from the words I'll say, the steps I'll take. It's stronger than thought, Philomela. I'm scared.

PHILOMELA   Oh, Procne, it's all right.

PROCNE   I know.

PHILOMELA   You'll be the queen of Thrace.

PROCNE   I know.

PHILOMELA   And after the wedding is over you can tell me the details.

PROCNE   I will.

PHILOMELA   You'll tell me everything I need to know and for that you'll be my hero. For that, you'll be my mother.

PROCNE   Philomela.

PHILOMELA   Now, let's try it again.

PROCNE   All right.

PHILOMELA   I'm Tereus.

PROCNE   All right.

                         As she speaks the ritual takes over.

                I, the untouched virgin,
                carry the basket down the secret steps of the Acropolis;
                down to the garden of Aphrodite,
                goddess of everything stroked and rubbed and wet.
                Down below like the virgin Persephone.
                Down to her fiery half-year home.
                Down to the grove below
                where the snake will crawl into the basket of Herse.

                         *Music starts as the ritual begins. PROCNE walks down the
                         steps of the Acropolis and enters the garden. She offers up
                         the basket and prays to Aphrodite. TEREUS appears, smiles
                         at PROCNE, picks her up and carries her off.*

                         The CHORUS steps out from the shadows.

YOUNG   I would have wished for a nuptial bed as splendid
                as that of Procne and Tereus,
                adorned with lilies and white tulle,
                surrounded by candles and the sumptuous scent
                of sweet pomegranate seeds.

BLEEDING   He stared at her for hours,
                every so often pulling back the sheet to have a look,
                then restraining himself knowing anticipation
                is the better part of satisfaction.

YOUNG   I would have wished for one just like it
                if I hadn't seen who made it.

DWINDLING   He watched her in the mirror at the side of the bed
                and as she looked to see him looking
                she caught sight of her own reflection:

pale, quivering, eager to dissolve the unknowing
that fluttered on her breath.

YOUNG   The furies made the bed and on the post perched an owl,
a dangerous sign of foreboding.

PIOUS   He kissed the tips of her fingers and the bottoms of her
feet.

PREGNANT   He leaned back to look in the mirror.

PIOUS   Again.

BLEEDING   He unwrapped her like the gift she had been,
and when he finally touched her breast
the owl cried out.

PIOUS   It shrieked through the night,
disrupting the pleasure of the newlyweds,
interrupting Tereus' concentration
so he couldn't fully enjoy his greatest reward
for a battle well-waged and won.

YOUNG   "Whoo whoo! Twit twoo!"

PIOUS   And curious Philomela standing at the door
thought she heard the cries of her sister in ecstasy:

Lights up on PHILOMELA.

PHILOMELA   Whoo whoo! Twit twoo!
That's the sound that lovers make.

PREGNANT   And then her sister was gone.
Off in a ship and across the sea
before Philomela had the chance
to be filled in on the details.

PHILOMELA puts a hand between her legs, masturbating.

PHILOMELA   Whoo whoo! Twit twoo. Whoo whoo.

PREGNANT   Philomela, annoyed and restless
with no one to count her sucked-in breath
tried to amuse herself.

PHILOMELA   Whoo whoo. Whoo whoo. I'm bored.

         Frustrated, she gives up.

PIOUS   Procne, on the other hand,
enchanted with the husband she was starting to love,
was nearly content with the birth of her very first child.

Scene 6 — Jaws of the Beast

         *The throne room in Thrace. PROCNE holds ITYS while
TEREUS plots a battle on his war map. During this scene
the CHORUS is present. The BLEEDING ONE plays the nurse
to ITYS and makes the sound of his laughter.*

         ITYS laughs.

PROCNE   He laughs like you.

TEREUS   Hmmm.

PROCNE   And his arms will hold great things like yours.

TEREUS   Where is my wingman?

PROCNE   But his eyes are just like Philomela's.

TEREUS   The strangest thing.

PROCNE   I said his eyes are like Philomela's.

TEREUS   Oh. Oh yes.

PROCNE   Look.

> *She passes the baby to* TEREUS. *He finds his soldier in the baby's grasp.* ITYS *laughs.*

TEREUS   He has it. Why didn't you say?

PROCNE   He wanted to show you himself.

TEREUS   Look at that.
Going to be a warrior like your father, I see.
Already gripping my wingman.
Where should Daddy put the wingman?
Close to the captain or by the back gate?

> ITYS *laughs. The baby puts the figure in his mouth.*

Into the jaws of the beast?
Then I will eat the beast!

> TEREUS *pretends to eat the baby.* PROCNE *and* ITYS *laugh.*

PROCNE   He chortles like you.

TEREUS   Grrrr.

PROCNE   He does.

> TEREUS *pretends to eat the baby again. The baby squeals.*

He squeals like you too.

TEREUS   I don't squeal.

PROCNE   I know how to make you squeal.

TEREUS   Grrrr.

They laugh.

PROCNE   But his eyes.

TEREUS   What's wrong with his eyes? Eyes like a warrior.

PROCNE   Eyes like Philomela.

TEREUS   Who?

PROCNE   My sister.

TEREUS   And what is my son doing with your sister's eyes?

PROCNE   Watching me.

TEREUS   Really?

PROCNE   Yes.

TEREUS   Watching your lips.

PROCNE   Yes.

TEREUS   Your neck.

PROCNE   Yes.

TEREUS   Your breasts.

PROCNE   Yes.

            Beat.

TEREUS   Let's see them.

PROCNE   Tereus.

TEREUS   Come on.

PROCNE   The baby.

TEREUS   He wants to see them too.
                Don't you, Itys.
                You want Mummy to bare her breasts.

> *ITYS laughs. TEREUS **hands the baby off** to the SERVANT
> while PROCNE **opens her dress**. TEREUS **sucks her breasts**.*

PROCNE   His eyes are like my sister's.

TEREUS   Nice little, round little, juicy little...

PROCNE   You wouldn't remember.

TEREUS   If her tits were like yours I'd remember.

PROCNE   Owch.

> *TEREUS **giggles like** ITYS. PROCNE **pushes him back**.*

TEREUS   That didn't hurt.

PROCNE   If you love me—

TEREUS   I won't bite again.

PROCNE   If you love me—

TEREUS   I'll chase you all over Thrace.

PROCNE   You'll bring my sister to visit.

TEREUS   I couldn't live without you for the journey there and back.

PROCNE   But then you can't see his eyes are just like her's.

TEREUS   Enough with the eyes.
                Who cares if his eyes are like your sister's?

PROCNE   Philomela.

TEREUS   If they are, then great, you can think of Philomela
             whenever your son is sucking on your tits but I'm not
             going all the way to Athens to look at your sister's eyes.

PROCNE   Fine.

TEREUS   Good.

PROCNE   All right.

TEREUS   Come here.

PROCNE   You'll drink me dry.

TEREUS   I know how to share.

             Beat.

             I'm preparing a campaign to the north.

PROCNE   You'll leave me.

TEREUS   We need to go soon, before Helios bakes us into sand.

PROCNE   For a war but not for my sister.

TEREUS   I'd go to Athens or anywhere else to make you happy but
             there just isn't time.

PROCNE   Only five days.

TEREUS   There. And five days back.

PROCNE   For me.

TEREUS   There just isn't time.

PROCNE   So you'll leave me in Thrace,
               in this palace where I don't know anyone,
               to start a war that wouldn't happen without your initiative,
               a war for your amusement, /
               but you refuse to —

TEREUS   War is not for my amusement.
               I need it like meat, like wine, like you.
               The battle's in my blood.

PROCNE   There is more than one way to boil your blood.

               She draws him to her.

               Take your battle out on me.
               Let me race your blood
               and then I'll send you down to Athens.

               PROCNE seduces TEREUS.

Scene 7 — Revenge

               *The BLEEDING ONE steps forward with the baby in her
               arms. TEREUS and PROCNE make love in the shadows.*

BLEEDING   Rage is in my blood, beating in my ears and tongue.
               It birthed itself in the clench of my jaw
               when I stumbled to the Safe Zone dressed as a man,
               passing women in the dirt
               with objects stuck up inside of them:
               a beer bottle, a golf club, a detonated firecracker.

               My stomach heaved with rage
               as I hid in the basement of the school,
               listening to the soldiers above
               dragging girls through the back doors,

loading them onto trucks:
pillaging the Safe Zone.

When I heard their boots on the stairs
I stuck my fingers down my throat and threw up.
I rubbed it on my face, in my hair
and collapsed myself on the floor.

When a soldier approached I groaned
and heaved myself forward.
He kicked me in the stomach
and moved on to the next.
Girl after girl they emptied the basement
until I was the only one left.

"What should I do with this one?"
the remaining soldier shouted up the stairs.
"Bring her up or run her through," was the reply.

He paced back and forth, examining me.
Back and forth, examining,
as rage curled my fingers to fists.

I leapt up, grabbed the bayonet from his belt
and backed against the wall.

He was surprised.
He was angry.
He seized my wrist and I bit him as hard as I could.
He cried out and other soldiers ran in
drawing their bayonets.

I lifted the soldier that held me
and used him as a shield against the others.
They stabbed him accidentally
and he screamed.

I laughed
until they gouged at my face,

at my eyes and my ears,
smashing my teeth
and piercing me eventually through the chest.

They stabbed me thirty-nine times,
raped me,
then left me for dead.
But they didn't bleed my rage.

> *TEREUS is asleep. PROCNE steps forward to take the child.*
> *The BLEEDING ONE talks directly to PROCNE.*

The blood—

PROCNE   Hmm?

BLEEDING   Blood is something you can't control.

PROCNE   No?

BLEEDING   It doesn't distinguish between love and war.

PROCNE   I'm the only one who gets to watch him sleep.

> *They look back at TEREUS sleeping. PROCNE returns to him.*
> *The CHORUS emerges slowly.*

BLEEDING   I am still bleeding now.
              I can't seem to stop bleeding.
              But when I do I'll join the army.
              I'll go back and kill the ones that killed me,
              stab them through with bayonets,
              cut off their pricks and nail them to trees and fences.

DWINDLING   The time will come,
              when our blood will boil with ambition
              and we will be the heroes of war.
              We will make valiant journeys home
              with many men in tow.

PIOUS   I will force my weapon into the mouth of a man
          and order him to get it up
          before I shoot him through the skull.
          Then I will slide down upon him like razor blades,
          the pressure overwhelming his skull,
          the shame caving in on his soul.

YOUNG   I will follow Artemis
          and make a fortress of my home.
          I will cut off my right breast like an Amazon
          to better draw my bow and shoot between the legs
          of every soldier that comes within range.

PREGNANT I will strangle him when he brags
          about putting babies in our bellies.
          He will play Niobe and I will hunt his children
          to avenge my mother's pride.

BLEEDING I will make him pay
          for everything he has done
          for everything he is doing
          for everything he will do.

          And you, you will do the same.

          CHORUS morphs back into the SLAVE WOMEN.

Scene 8 — The Request

          *PANDION's throne room in Athens. TEREUS appeals to
          PANDION while PHILOMELA, hiding, listens to their
          conversation. The SLAVE WOMEN attend PANDION.*

PANDION   You already have one of my daughters.

TEREUS   And that daughter implores you,
          she begs, Your Highness.

PANDION   Bring in the meat.

TEREUS   Procne is desperate for her sister.

               The meat is brought. PANDION *eats.*

               Sir?

PANDION   Any more battles then?

TEREUS   Last month I took on the Spartans.

PANDION   The Spartans!
               They fatten and eat their prisoners of war.

TEREUS   They took no prisoners from Thrace.

PANDION   You'd think they were swinging from trees, those Spartans.

TEREUS   Yes. Now, I should / get back—

PANDION   Eating prisoners. Ha!
               That's a way to get sick.
               What do you do with yours?

TEREUS   Mine?

PANDION   Your prisoners of war.

TEREUS   Bring back the women and children as slaves
               and dispense with the men.

PANDION   Their heads at least.

TEREUS   Yes, their heads.

PANDION   Ha! *(beat)* Shouldn't you ask me?

TEREUS   Ask you?

PANDION   What we do with our prisoners.

TEREUS   Of course. *(beat)* What do you do with your prisoners?

PANDION   We test them for literacy.

TEREUS   Literacy?

PANDION   Those who can read work as scribes,
copying the greatest literature of our time.
Have you seen my library, then?

TEREUS   No.

PANDION   I have twenty-five copies of Hesiod's *Theogony*.

TEREUS   Wonderful.

PANDION   Three hundred and twelve prisoners have gone blind!

TEREUS   Impressive.

PANDION   Now that's civilized.
That's what the civilized do with prisoners of war.

TEREUS   On the subject or war, sir, I should tell you I'm set to wage
a campaign to the north.

PANDION   The north?

TEREUS   Yes.

PANDION   The hot days are coming.

TEREUS   Which is why I really should return to Thrace.

PANDION   Yes.

TEREUS   As soon as I receive your consent.

PANDION   Consent?

TEREUS   To bring Philomela with me to visit her sister.

PANDION   Wine.

TEREUS   Procne implores you, sir,
                 but if the answer is no, I should set sail at once.

                 TEREUS starts to exit. PHILOMELA appears.

PHILOMELA   No. Don't go.

PANDION   Back to your studies, luv.

PHILOMELA   Oh Father, please, I'm sunken without my sister.

TEREUS   This is the sister?

PANDION   You are your mother and sister combined.

PHILOMELA   Father, please.

TEREUS   The sister I met before?

PHILOMELA   Look at me, Father, look at my sad countenance.
                 See how dour I've become.

PANDION   Yes, yes, mopey little thing.

PHILOMELA   I cry every night thinking of Procne so far away.

TEREUS   And Procne cries for you;
                 for your soft beauty and... for... sisterhood.

PHILOMELA   But when I think of going with Tereus,
                 look what happens to my face.

TEREUS   The glow of a goddess.

PHILOMELA   My eyes are stars sparkling into your skies.
               My cheeks are the sun,
               rising up into your beautiful morning.
               My voice is a brook,
               gurgling into your forest, Father.

PANDION   Would you listen to this then.

PHILOMELA   Look at how happy I am, Father,
               when I think of going with Tereus.

PANDION   When you think of leaving me.

PHILOMELA   Only to return with this glow, this love, this laughter.
               Oh, when I think of going with Tereus,
               I want to dance and sing.

               She grabs TEREUS *and whirls him about.*

PANDION   So now you get a taste.

TEREUS   A taste?

PANDION   Of this persuasive little cat.

TEREUS   Oh, yes.

PANDION   How would you feel with this minx aboard your ship?

TEREUS   Very... good.

PHILOMELA   Then I can go?

PANDION   Well...

PHILOMELA   Father, Daddy, please, please,
               I love you, Father, Daddy, please.

TEREUS   Gentle King, I must tell you, once again,

how Procne sickens to be so far away from her sister.
She lies in bed at night and moans
for the soft sororal comfort only Philomela can bring.
Please, King, have pity on Procne,
so far away from home;
have pity on Philomela,
longing for her closest friend;
and have pity on me, a mere slave to them both.

He cries.

PANDION   Are you... are you crying, man?

PHILOMELA   He's crying, yes. I think he's crying.

PANDION   Well, pull yourself in then.

TEREUS   It is Procne's longing that has affected me so.

PHILOMELA   Please, Father, let Tereus take me.

TEREUS   Her safety will be my highest priority.

PANDION   Well then, well, then, all right.
But only for a month or two.

PHILOMELA   Thank you, Father, thank you.

PANDION   Come home soon, luv.

PHILOMELA   I will.

PANDION   Soon.

PANDION exits.

Scene 9 — The Journey

YOUNG   And so the ship set sail.

> *PHILOMELA runs up and down the deck of TEREUS' ship, drinking in the sea air.*

PHILOMELA   Crybaby, crybaby!

TEREUS   I do what needs to be done.

PHILOMELA   The tears were planned?

TEREUS   Not planned.

PHILOMELA   You are under the spell of Procne.

TEREUS   That must be it.

PHILOMELA   I hope my husband will love me like that.

TEREUS   He won't be able to hold himself back.

PHILOMELA   I haven't been from the palace in so long.
And then, just with my father
or those whining slaves.

TEREUS   No freedom?

PHILOMELA   I'm always bored.

TEREUS   You should have stolen a boat and come to visit us.

PHILOMELA   The breeze is so fresh and the dolphins —
Look! The dolphins are racing the boat.

TEREUS   Let's see.

PHILOMELA   There. Look.

                He steps behind her, puts his hands around her waist.

TEREUS   I see.

PHILOMELA   Yes.

TEREUS   I see.

                Beat.

                Has a man ever put his hands around your waist?

PHILOMELA   No.

TEREUS   I don't want you to fall.

PHILOMELA   I know.

TEREUS   You don't mind?

PHILOMELA   I don't mind.

TEREUS   Is that a blush I see rising up in your cheek?

PHILOMELA   Procne must love to go out on the sea.

TEREUS   A little touch of pink?

PHILOMELA   Or does she prefer to stay at home
                with your son?

TEREUS   Do you feel shy around me?

PHILOMELA   Tell me everything about Procne.

TEREUS   You'll see her soon enough.

PHILOMELA   Look, Brother, there,
                       the dolphins leap up from the sea.

TEREUS   I asked them to welcome you.

PHILOMELA   You did not.

TEREUS   They never leap up for me.

YOUNG   When the ship came to shore,
                       Tereus sat Philomela on a horse
                       and rode her into the forest, alone.
                       Deep and down and into a private hunting cabin
                       with thick walls and a lock on the door.

Scene 10 — The Unexpected

> TEREUS *closes the door of the hunting cabin.* PHILOMELA
> *is confused.*

TEREUS   I feel it in my teeth first.
                       Always in my teeth—like chewing metal.
                       Some people have wise blood but mine is wild,
                       like a wolf or a lion.

PHILOMELA   Can I see my sister?

TEREUS   I know when it's going to happen but
                       why does it start in my teeth?

PHILOMELA   Please?

TEREUS   An aching from inside my teeth
                       and a watering at the mouth,
                       a throbbing in the fist.
                       It's a clenching in my jaw
                       and on the underside of my skull

until I see it:
skin.

PHILOMELA   It's cold in here.

TEREUS   I don't want to caress it.
             I don't want to lick it.
             I want to bite it, stick iron into it,
             slice it into pieces
             and pin it up around me.
             It's my blood, not me,
             my blood and my teeth.

PHILOMELA   Why don't we go and see Procne.

             She moves to leave; he stops her.

TEREUS   When I saw you,
             my blood wanted to grab you by the waist,
             by the face and carry you off.
             And when I saw your cheek in your father's hand,
             I wanted to cut off that hand,
             put my blood in its place—
             I was so jealous of his proximity
             to you.

PHILOMELA   Please.

TEREUS   You look like a nymph alone in a stream of my blood.
             Are you afraid of me?

PHILOMELA   No.

TEREUS   Whilst I waited for you to pack your things
             I fuelled my blood with the memory of your lips,
             your teeth, your hands, your feet and every part of you
             that had been covered with cloth.

PHILOMELA   No.

TEREUS   And it's my blood, right now, you understand /

PHILOMELA   No.

TEREUS   It's my blood that grabs at your ankle /

PHILOMELA   No.

TEREUS   Claws up your knee /

PHILOMELA   No.

TEREUS   My blood that tears at your dress,
unfastens, unhooks, unbuttons
and strips layers and layers of clothing.
It's my blood that will not be deterred
by the grip of your bodice to your breasts,
that bites at your nipples and squeezes your neck.
It's my boiled blood that does it.
It's my wild blood squeezing your wrists above your head
with my knee to your belly and my voice screaming:

shut up shut up shut up you bitch look at your messy hair
your dirty face your red pocked cheeks you whore you cunt
you less than human it's my blood and you can't blame me
for that so stop looking at me with venom you snake you
minx you tempted me you wanted me to yank your hair and
fuck fuck fuck you whore it's your cunt tit back spit tears
snot thighs juice cum BLOOD BLOOD BLOOD IT'S MY BLOOD—

He cums.

Long beat.

PHILOMELA   I don't care about your blood.
I don't care about your blood.

You've dropped me like something half-eaten.
Don't you see me suffer?
Look at me.

Look at me under the mess you've made all over my skin.
Ewwwwwwwww.
I'll scrape this flesh from my arms
and yank this hair from my head for shame of you.
Shame.
Look at me.
Now.
Look at me.
I'm ugly, I'm empty,
I am the remnants of myself.

TEREUS   It's my blood.

PHILOMELA   I don't care,
I don't care about your blood.
I'm ruined like they said I could be ruined
and now I am nothing because I have wounds from you
all over me.

TEREUS   My blood.

PHILOMELA   And what about my blood?
What about me?
You've dragged us here:
my father, my sister, my body, your son,
all of us are me scraping my skin into dirt telling everyone
of the shame you've forced into me.
Why didn't you kill me first?
Get your blood raged up in murder rather than this.

TEREUS   Shut up.

PHILOMELA   At least then my soul could rest
without the knowledge of this.

TEREUS   Shut up.

PHILOMELA   Kill me now.

TEREUS   Shut up / shut up—

PHILOMELA   Open my throat and bleed me out through two holes at once.
              One is not enough to take this pain.
              Not enough.

TEREUS   Shut your mouth.

PHILOMELA   You will answer for this.
              The gods watch all evil and if they are more than names
              they will see me.
              See me!
              See me down here scraping my shame deeper into my wounds.
              See me! See me / see me see me see me see me.

TEREUS   Shut up shut up shut up / shut up shut up—

PHILOMELA   I won't stop screaming.
              I won't stop saying the words
              again and again and again.
              Rape! Rape! Rape!

                     He seizes her.

              Do it.
              Cut my throat.
              Do it.
              Coward.

                     He cuts out her tongue. PHILOMELA *falls to the floor.* PROCNE
                     enters as though in the palace upon TEREUS' *return.*

TEREUS   Oh Procne, Procne, oh.
              I don't know how I will ever forgive myself.
              Your sister was standing at the prow of the ship,
              leaning over the rail to watch the dolphins race and play.
              "Step away, my sister, step away from the bow."
              She mocked my serious tone
              and just then we fell from the crest of a wave.
              Philomela, the dear child, she toppled into the sea.
              She must have hit her head on the side of the boat

for though a dozen men or more dove down after her,
we could not find Philomela.
Procne, I'm so ashamed.
I'm racked with guilt that I couldn't better protect her.
I'm sorry.
I am.
I'm so sorry.

PROCNE exits. TEREUS rapes PHILOMELA again.

Scene 11 — Trapped

The CHORUS steps forward. As they speak, TEREUS continues to rape PHILOMELA.

PIOUS   At times like these when we are pounded
             into earth and muck and slime,
             we look up from where we lay and think:

DWINDLING   If we were birds we could fly up,

YOUNG   Away from this wrenching pain,

PREGNANT   Away from the shame and the blood and the terror,

YOUNG   Away from what will be left of ourselves when he's done.

DWINDLING   If we were birds he would disappear below
             as the wind caught our wings like sails.

BLEEDING   Up up up we'd go, into clouds
             where our hearts could beat as loudly as they are.

PIOUS   If we were birds.

CHORUS   If we were birds.

TEREUS exits.

YOUNG	They kept me tied to a stake in the ground, on a bed of leaves under plastic sheeting.
DWINDLING	Every night they pulled me from the cellar.
PREGNANT	Six of them on me, taking turns, in my own bed.
DWINDLING	Like a rat, they pulled me out.
BLEEDING	I was in the Safe Zone.
PREGNANT	They made my husband watch.
PIOUS	I was taken to an internment camp.
PREGNANT	He threw up, poor thing.
PIOUS	They kept us in empty rooms that used to be classrooms.
DWINDLING	Some hid in attics.
PIOUS	At night they would come with flashlights, shine them in our faces.
BLEEDING	Some in roofs of barns.
PIOUS	We tried not to be seen because we knew they would grab one or two girls who would never come back.
YOUNG	Some hid in holes in the manioc fields.
BLEEDING	Some hid in piles of bodies.
PIOUS	The night they grabbed me, I was whispering prayers to the girls around me: "Please god please god please god please."

They took me to a room
where there were seven soldiers.
They elbowed two young ones
who had caps pulled over their faces.
I knew those two.
They had been my neighbours before the ethnic cleansing began.

CHORUS   Please god please god please god please.

PIOUS   They gave the boys drinks
and told them to rape me,
to enjoy it,
to complete their initiation.
The first boy grinned as though our eyes had never met.
He tore the clothes from my body
and raped me on a table while the older men cheered.
When he was done,
he spit in my face.

CHORUS   Please god please god.

PIOUS   The other boy squirmed.
He made awkward jokes,
he made excuses.
A soldier hit him in the head,
another fired a shot into the ceiling.

They made me undress him,
the boy who had been my neighbour.
He was thin and trembling.
Tears welled in his eyes.
They made me touch him and pull him into me.
They chanted, jeered, threatened if he didn't "get it up"
they'd shoot him in the head.
I whispered in his ear:
"Good boy, you can do it, good boy, come on."

He couldn't get it up but I pretended that he did.

PIOUS & CHORUS
 Good boy, you can do it, good boy, come on.

PIOUS   They shot him while he wept
          and sent me back to the room.

YOUNG   Oh, Philomela, banished to the room.

PIOUS   The room of remembering the face of that boy.

BLEEDING The room of bleeding and wringing of hands.

PIOUS   The room of praying for others like him.

DWINDLING The room of eternal captivity.

PIOUS   The room in which despair can give way to hope,
          or maybe a chance at escape.

PREGNANT If there was something sharp,
          something heavy,
          something in the ceiling to hang yourself from, you would.

DWINDLING But there is nothing,
          in this room,
          there is nothing.

PIOUS   But a loom.
          A Thracian loom with dirty thread lying in a tangled heap.

          PHILOMELA crawls toward the loom.

          Philomela, you can crawl
          toward life outside this room.

          PHILOMELA weaves.

Scene 12 — Mourning in Athens

> *PANDION is wheeled into his throne room by the SLAVE WOMEN.*
> *They cater to his every need. The YOUNG ONE SW sings.*

YOUNG SW   (*singing*) The king is crying, sobbing, weeping;
Now the rivers overflow.
My fields are flooded, cattle drowned,
Prayers are sinking with my land.

The king is angry, fuming, raging;
Now the city shakes with fear.
My fields are scorched, my cattle starving,
Prayers are endless yet unheard.

I am crying, angry, lonely;
Life goes on the way it has.
No one stops to soothe my pain.
Life goes on the way it has.
Life goes on...

> *PANDION applauds.*

PANDION   Luv, my little luv.
Come and sit by me.

YOUNG SW   Yes, Father.

PANDION   Talent like that doesn't spring from the earth.

YOUNG SW   It must have come from somewhere.

PANDION   Your mother, I tell you, the voice of a nymph.

YOUNG SW   Are my eyes like hers?

PANDION   Your eyes and your ears.

YOUNG SW	And my nose and my lips, are they like hers too?
PANDION	You, my luv, are the spitting image of your mother. And your sister... your sister...
YOUNG SW	The one you sent away?
PREGNANT SW	The one you married off?
BLEEDING SW	The one who gave birth to a grandchild that you have never seen?
PANDION	Wine. More wine!
PIOUS SW	Father, I should mention—
PANDION	Girls, my girls.
PIOUS SW	Your advisors wish to see you.
PANDION	Look at your lovely new clothes.
PIOUS SW	They are threatening to break down the door.
PANDION	Another song.
PIOUS SW	And the king of Thebes has just arrived.
PANDION	Or a dance, let's have a dance.

PANDION tries to stand and dance.

PIOUS SW	He wishes to know, Father, why you have cut off trade routes to and from Athens.
PANDION	Ba ba ba.
PIOUS SW	He wants to know why you have sent word for all Athenians to return at once and banished foreign nationals from the city.

PANDION	Ba ba ba ba...
PIOUS SW	He wants to know why you have refused consent for any ship to set sail from your harbour and prohibited any foreign ship from docking. He wants to know, Father, why you are reinforcing the city's walls.

PANDION sits.

PANDION	And what business is it of his.
PIOUS SW	He suspects you are preparing for war.
PANDION	For war!
PIOUS SW	Yes, Father, for war.
PANDION	And is that what you suspect?
PIOUS SW	I suspect you have a reason for everything you do.
PANDION	That's right.
PIOUS SW	And it's not for the king of Thebes to question your authority.
PANDION	It's not for him, no, that's right.
PIOUS SW	Especially after you so generously came to his defence.
PANDION	I saved his life. I saved his city. I sent an army to... A warrior to—
PREGNANT SW	To take both your daughters away?
PANDION	Wine. Please. Wine.

DWINDLING SW   When he came back to ask for more,
                why did you give in?

PANDION   Wine.

PIOUS SW   Why did you give in?

PANDION   International relations are a complicated thing.

BLEEDING SW   It was a matter of trade?

PANDION   They need to be maintained—trust is required.

DWINDLING SW   It was a matter of economy?

PANDION   There are ways for things to be done.

PREGNANT SW   A diplomatic consolation?

PANDION   He wouldn't take no for an answer
               and you were so desperate to go.

DWINDLING SW   How could you say no?

PANDION   I protect. It's my job to protect. Protect money, protect
               food, protect health and well-being.

YOUNG SW   Then why didn't you protect me?

PANDION   Protect you?

PREGNANT SW   You told me to board that ship.

PANDION   But I didn't want you to go.

BLEEDING SW   You told me to leave with Tereus.

PANDION   He promised to take good care—

DWINDLING SW   Why did you want me to go?

PANDION   I didn't want—

BLEEDING SW   Why did you send me away?

PANDION   My luv—

YOUNG SW   You threw me into the sea.

PANDION   My luv—

CHORUS   You threw me into the sea.

PANDION   I threw my daughter into the sea!

        Beat.

PIOUS SW   And what should I tell the king?

PANDION   The king?

PIOUS SW   The king of Thebes.

PANDION   Everything from Athens will stay in Athens.
               Nothing comes in, nothing goes out.
               There is no more leaving to be done.

Scene 13 — Procne's Revelation

        ITYS giggles. TEREUS enters looking for the two-year-old child.

TEREUS   All right, little soldier. Nurse says it's time for your bath.

        ITYS giggles.

Come out come out wherever you are.

PROCNE enters for her mourning ritual.

PROCNE   Don't get him excited before bed.

ITYS giggles.

TEREUS   Gotcha!

TEREUS pounces on the child offstage. ITYS erupts in fits of giggles. PROCNE sighs and begins her ritual.

PROCNE   Poseidon, care for my sister in your watery depths.
Wrap her in coral and soft sea growth.
Make a shrine of her grave
that when fish swim by,
they are warmed by her sweet soft sigh.

The SERVANT enters and clears her throat.

What is it?

SERVANT   I'm sorry to interrupt your daily ritual, my lady.

PROCNE   Make it quick.

SERVANT   If you knew what I had to give, you wouldn't be so quick to speed me out.

PROCNE   Fine.

SERVANT   May I just ask one small favour before I give you what you have to look forward to receiving?

PROCNE   Just give it to me.

SERVANT   Of course, my lady. I just... well first off... I just wouldn't mind a little assurance, or reassurance, for the predicted outcome of your reaction or response or retort to the said

	object I bring because I know your lady, understandably, has become irritable—no, sorry—short-tempered—no, sorry—touchy, perhaps, since her sister's unfortunate drowning and I...
PROCNE	Are you trying to stay my temper with babble?
SERVANT	Oh, uh, I hadn't thought of it that way. Let me see, no, no I don't think so. I was just hoping that if what I have to give pleases, you might remember how carefully I concealed it and brought it to you.
PROCNE	Fine.
SERVANT	Stuffed it up my shirt: "Look at me, I'm pregnant!" But, uh, also, maybe, if what I have doesn't please you, then you'll remember I'm just a homely messenger who has very exciting plans this evening for the Bacchae celebration, and I've nothing in my head but blablablablabla.

> PROCNE *puts out her hand. The servant zips her mouth and passes the parcel to* PROCNE. *It is a white sheet—the tapestry.*

PROCNE	What is it?
SERVANT	It's a tapestry.
PROCNE	I know it's a tapestry but where did you get it?
SERVANT	From my cousin's wife who's been serving in silence somewhere in the woods. My cousin says it's a spirit she serves, with one foot in, one foot out of Hades.

> PROCNE *and the* SERVANT *stretch out the tapestry. Lighting shift: the sheet is lit from behind.*

> *Movement piece: silhouetted tableaux of the rape and dismemberment are projected onto the tapestry.* PROCNE *understands every image.*

Some excellent needlework. A bit gory for the boy's room, maybe, but I suppose it's a little cathartic.

PROCNE   When do the rites begin?

SERVANT   Rites?

PROCNE   To Bacchus.

SERVANT   Oh, those rites. Sundown, of course.

PROCNE   Please inform my husband that I will be joining in the uproar.

SERVANT   You will?

PROCNE   It's not every day a woman can get possessed by a god's drunken frenzy and run screaming into the forest.

SERVANT   Ah... yes, I mean, no. Yes.

          The SERVANT exits. PROCNE is alone.

PROCNE   I cannot conjure a drop of grief
          from the pit of my stomach to my eyes or my tongue.
          I am numb with ruin.
          My skin cannot remember what it is to touch,
          to be touched.

          Why have you done this?
          Why have you done this to her?
          Why have you done this to me?
          Husband?

          My thoughts are consumed with revenge,
          dipped in oil and set alight I burn with it.
          I burn with it now, with revenge.
          Revenge.

Scene 14 — The Rescue

The CHORUS beats the thyrsus on the ground, cymbals rattle and the worshipers call. The celebration to Bacchus begins.

Music and movement piece/dance: the worshipers, played by the CHORUS, arrive in a frenzy. PROCNE disguises herself as a worshiper and dances into the forest with the women. She searches through the forest until she discovers the cabin with PHILOMELA inside. PROCNE disguises her sister and rescues her from the cabin. They return to the palace where PROCNE reveals herself to her terrified sister. The worshipers disappear into the night.

Scene 15 — The Reunion

PROCNE   Sister. Sister.

               PROCNE tries to embrace PHILOMELA but she twists away. PHILOMELA stares at the floor in shame.

I didn't know.
I didn't know.

I knew he needed...
I knew he had to...
I thought there was a difference between family and war.
I'm sorry.
I'm so sorry.

Listen to me.
Listen with those ears that heard
the screams of your ravaged tongue.
Tears won't help us.
Prayers won't help us.

Nothing but the sword will help us,
the sword or something worse,
if it can be found, then something worse to punish him
for this merciless attack.

Look at me, Sister.
Look at me with those eyes
that have watched the blood stream from your body.
I am as hard as rock, as unflinching as iron
and nothing will prevent me from inflicting
such enormous pain upon that tyrant, Tereus.

That name, it burns in my mouth and throat
and I cannot spit it out.
I will break his bones one by one,
stick needles through his swollen joints,
and hack away at his limbs,
chopping, or twisting, or burning.

I'll hang him from his tongue
like a fish on a hook
and let him dangle till the weight of it
sends him plummeting to earth,
until his soul is screaming, unhinged
and desperate for the underworld.
And I will follow him everywhere, torturing.
Torturing.

Feel me, Sister.
Feel the strength in these arms
that once held Tereus gently, but now pulse with wrath.
Hear the resolve of these lips:
this revenge will make the very earth gape in horror.

> *The SERVANT enters.*

SERVANT   My lady. *(beat)* Excuse me.

PROCNE   What is it?

SERVANT	I apologize but Itys will not go down for his nap without a kiss.
PROCNE	A kiss?
SERVANT	Yes, my lady.
PROCNE	A kiss from me.
SERVANT	I wouldn't have thought it appropriate to disturb your lady but you know how persuasive that monkey can be. Such a sweet little thing and my heart just melts when he asks me politely to fetch his mummy so he'll be assured of the sweetest dreams.
PROCNE	In a minute.
SERVANT	I didn't mean to / intrude.
PROCNE	I'll be there in a minute.

The SERVANT exits. PROCNE looks at PHILOMELA.

Itys is the mirror image of his father.
Except for his eyes.
They are yours, Philomela.

Scene 16 — The Bloody Deed

The SERVANT stands in the doorway with ITYS.

ITYS	Mummy.
PROCNE	They are yours.
ITYS	Mummy.
PROCNE	Bring him in.

PROCNE takes the child in her arms.

PREGNANT   The boy wrapped his small arms
             around his mother's neck;
             kissing and giggling,
             whining and whispering:

ITYS   Mummy mummy mummy.

DWINDLING   But with tears sucked down her throat
             Procne dragged the boy to a murky,
             unused room in the palace;
             her mad-looking sister trailing behind.

ITYS   Mummy.

PROCNE   Be still.

ITYS   Mummy.

CHORUS   *(whispered)* Be still, be still.

PROCNE   In childbirth you launched such pain through my body.
             I bit a stick in two and squeezed the hand of my midwife
             until her scream could rival mine.
             You brought me to the precipice of agony
             until I thought I might die.

ITYS   Mummy—

CHORUS   Be still / be still be still be still.

PROCNE   Then to see your tiny features,
             your ears, your toes, your red-faced screech
             soothed only at my breast,
             my heart swelled with love
             until I thought I might die.

She kisses him and hugs him too tightly.

You are still mine now
but soon you will be his; all his.
Look at you.
Your hands already ache to command a weapon,
your blood simmers,
yearning to maim and kill and rape.

CHORUS   Be still / be still be still be still.

PROCNE   One day you will hold a woman down
who will never again be able to stand,
a woman whose tongue will rot on the ground,
whose heart will throb with agony.

Then you will die in battle at the hands of a stranger.
Is it not better I should spare you the pain
of dying alone by the sword of one who knows you not?

ITYS   Mummy?

CHORUS   Be still.

PROCNE   He is not a child but a part of myself;
an extra limb I've coddled from birth.
The love I have for him is not the love
from one person to another,
rather the love I have for my arm or my leg
or any other part of myself.

ITYS   Mummy?

CHORUS   Be still / be still. (continues until murder)

PROCNE   Do I not have the right to sever that which is part of my
own body?

ITYS   Mummy?

PROCNE   To dismember that limb which has become
cankerous and infected?

ITYS   Mummy?

PROCNE   To remove a festering growth
                that lives as a reminder I have been loved and groped
                and devoured by a beast?

ITYS   Mummy?

PROCNE   By a monster?

ITYS   Mummy mummy / mummy mummy mummy mummy...

PROCNE   Be still be still be still be still be still be still.

> PROCNE *kills* ITYS. *Long beat.*

PIOUS   Then the sisters, like a strange coven,
                tore pulsating chunks of flesh from the boy's tiny frame,
                and threw them into brass pots
                where they sizzled in their own fat.

BLEEDING   Some flesh they cooked over an open flame,
                of the entrails they made a stew
                and of the liver, a chalky pâté.

PREGNANT   And then.

DWINDLING   And then.

YOUNG   And then.

CHORUS   Tereus came to supper.

Scene 17 — Supper Time

> TEREUS *kisses* PROCNE.

TEREUS   What an exhausting day I've had.

PROCNE   Oh?

TEREUS   Breaking in the new recruits.
                I really do question the way
                Thracians are raising their sons these days.

PROCNE   They're too soft?

TEREUS   Soft as goat's cheese.

PROCNE   The parents are to blame.

TEREUS   Where is everyone?

PROCNE   It will just be the two of us this evening.

TEREUS   Oh?

PROCNE   It's an Athenian tradition
                in which a wife serves her husband
                without the aid of a servant.

TEREUS   I don't know how Athenians manage to get anything done
                with all their bloody traditions.
                What's this?

PROCNE   A seven-dish spread.

TEREUS   And you cooked it yourself?

PROCNE   Sample each one.

TEREUS   Or we could take advantage of this time alone.

                    He pulls her toward him. She sits him down.

PROCNE   Maybe after you're nice and full.

                    *He sits and scoops up some food. He starts to bring it to his
                    mouth.*

TEREUS   Come sit next to me then.

PROCNE   Of course.

> *She sits next to him. He smiles. He starts to bring it to his mouth then offers the food to her.*

TEREUS   Shouldn't the cook have the first taste?

PROCNE   The wife doesn't eat until her husband is finished.

TEREUS   That doesn't seem fair.

PROCNE   Eat. Please.

> *He does.*

Do you like it?

TEREUS   We'll have to get you into the kitchen more often.

PROCNE   Spread this one on some bread.

TEREUS   Mmmmm.

PROCNE   Good?

TEREUS   It's not just the way they handle their weapons.

PROCNE   Pardon me?

TEREUS   More essentially, their lack of resilience and inner fortitude. Would you believe three of them started weeping at the end of the training day? They said it was the dust and sun in their eyes but I'm quite confident it was a strong case of Missing Mummy. Mmmm, this one's good.

PROCNE   Yes.

TEREUS   That's why I'm at you to be tough with Itys. I know he's
                your only son but you really need to stop coddling him.
                That boy needs to learn how to be independent, strong-
                willed and thick-skinned.

PROCNE   How about this one.

TEREUS   I can't eat eyeballs.

PROCNE   You'll like these.

TEREUS   I feel them staring right at me.

                She feeds him an eyeball: crunch.

                Mmm.
                Where is Itys anyway?
                Doesn't he get to eat with his father?
                Bring him in.

PROCNE   He's already in.

TEREUS   Where?

PROCNE   He's closer to you now than he could possibly be.

                TEREUS looks under his chair.

TEREUS   Some sort of Athenian game?

PROCNE   Itys! Your father wants to see you.

                *PHILOMELA enters with ITYS' eyeless head. The CHORUS
                steps forward, breathing audibly with the pace of the scene.*

TEREUS   What the hell is... what the hell...
                No no no no no.
                I am the grave of my son?

He tries to throw up.

You you you you
you you you you
YOU YOU YOU YOU—

ALL   AHHHHHHHHH!

> *All scream until they run out of breath. They are suspended.*
> *They breathe.*

Epilogue

PHILOMELA   At that moment, we were all three suspended.
               In our terror,
               in our grief,
               in our pain,
               in our longing,
               in our guilt;
               stretched out in anguish until...
               until...
               until...

ALL   We were birds.

PROCNE   My lips pursed to a hardened point.

TEREUS   My limbs shrunk in uncomfortable proportions.

PHILOMELA   I saw further to the left, further to the right, a widening
               of periphery.

PROCNE   And this twitch.

PHILOMELA   Yes, this twitch began to flicker in my neck.

PROCNE   The gods made us birds.

TEREUS   All of us.

PHILOMELA   Up and round the throne room, through the window
             flapping with might and regret.

CHORUS   We were birds, yes,

PHILOMELA   We were birds.

PIOUS   But it wasn't the escape we had dreamed.

PREGNANT   Our thoughts fly above the earth,

YOUNG   But we will never reach the sky,

DWINDLING   Because we're always reliving the pain.

BLEEDING   Human reason trapped in animal body.

TEREUS   Ever hunting,

PROCNE   Ever hunted,

CHORUS   Always hungry.

PHILOMELA   And it's awful.
             It's brutish and painful and gory
             and the memories are forever wedged in our thoughts.
             There is no escape or release.
             I will always be living the horror
             of what has been done,
             of what I have done,
             but still
             I continue to fly.
             Still we continue to fly.

Acknowledgements

In addition to everyone who worked on the production, I would like to thank the following people and organizations who were integral to the play's development:

Dramaturges Alan Dilworth, Andrea Romaldi, Richard Rose and Vicki Stroich; actors Rose Cortez, Edwige Jean-Pierre and Ieva Lucs; the SummerWorks Theatre Festival, Alberta Theatre Projects, the Ontario Arts Council and the Toronto Arts Council.

author photo by Ian Brown

Erin Shields is a Toronto-based playwright and actor who trained at the Rose Bruford College of Speech and Drama in London, England. She is a founding member of Groundwater Productions, through which she creates and develops most of her work, including *If We Were Birds*, which was produced by the Tarragon Theatre in 2010. The production received five Dora Mavor Moore nominations and won for Best Actress and Sound Design. Other works include *Montparnasse*, winner of the Alberta Theatre Projects' Enbridge Emerging playRites Award, produced by Groundwater Productions in association with Theatre Passe Muraille; *The Epic of Gilgamesh* (Groundwater/SummerWorks), the Dora-nominated *The Unfortunate Misadventures of Masha Galinski* (Groundwater/Canadian Tour) and *Dance of the Red Skirts* (Theatre Columbus). Erin is also a playwright-in-residence at Tarragon Theatre.